The big 5
and other wild animals

Buffalo
Megan Emmett

The big 5 and other wild animals series is published by
Awareness Publishing Group (Pty) Ltd.
Copyright © 2019

Awareness Publishing (SA) (Pty) Ltd
www.awareness.co.za
info@awareness.co.za
+27 (0)86 110 1491
www.facebook.com/AwarenessPublishing

All rights reserved. No part of this publication may be reproduced in any form without written permission from the publisher, except by a reviewer.

First edition, 2019

Buffalo by Megan Emmett
ISBN 978-0-6393-0005-4

Summary: An introduction to the buffalo, one of the Big Five wild animals. This book looks at the buffalo's family life and daily activities, its physical characteristics, buffalo babies and more.

Book design: Dana Espag and Bianca Keenan-Smith.

Editorial credits: Educational consultant: Gillian Mervis. Copy editor: Danya Ristić. Proofreader: Lynda Gilfillan. Picture editor: Anne Laing. Indexer: Lois C Henderson.

Illustrations: Cartoons: Gerhard Cruywagen of Greenhouse Cartoons, and Dana Espag.

Photo credits: Cover and pp.3 (top and bottom), 6, 9 (bottom), 18, 36 (top), and 40 © Anne Laing; pp.3 (middle), 19 (middle), 25, 36 (bottom), and 37 (left) © Shem Compion; p.4 © palko72 / Shutterstock; pp.7, 16, 19 (left), 27 and 38 © Megan Emmett; p.8 © David Steele / Shutterstock; p.9 (top) © Peter Betts / Shutterstock; p.10 © Michael Sheehan / Shutterstock; p.11 © RainervonBrandis / iStockphoto; p.12 © Ecoimages / Shutterstock; p.13 © MartinMaritz / Shutterstock; p.14 © lexan / Shutterstock; p.15 © TierImage / iStockphoto; p.19 (right) © David Steele / Shutterstock; p.20 © Stefanie van der Vinden / Shutterstock; p.22 © WA van den Noort / Shutterstock; p.24 © hilton123 / iStockphoto; p.26 © Ewan Chesser / Shutterstock; p.28 © Mogens Trolle / Shutterstock; p.30 © Mitsuaki Iwago / Gallo Images; p.31 © Pete Oxford / Gallo Images; p.32 © Four Oaks / Shutterstock; p.33 (top, middle and bottom) © Four Oaks / Shutterstock; p.34 © Four Oaks / Shutterstock; p.35 © pjmalsbury / iStockphoto; p.37 (middle) © hedrus / Shutterstock; (right) © pjmalsbury / iStockphoto.

You can read more by Megan Emmett about animals in the book *Game Ranger in Your Backpack – All-in-one Interpretative Guide to the Lowveld*, published by Briza Publications (2010, Pretoria). ISBN 978-1-920217-06-8.

1 3 5 7 9 0 8 6 4 2

Contents

Quick facts 5
Meet the buffalo 7
Males and females 9
Food 11
Drinking water 13
Family life – herds 15
Family life – clans 17
Who is the boss? 19
Fighting 21
Finding the way 23
Old buffalo bulls 25
Senses 27
Beating the heat 29
Protecting the herd 31
Flehmen 33
Baby buffalo 35
Buffalo and birds 37
Glossary 39

A herd of African buffalo.

Quick facts

Height (at the shoulder)	1,4 metres
Weight	Males: 800 kilograms Females: 750 kilograms
Lifespan	About 23 years
Gestation (pregnancy)	11 months
Number of young	One at a time
Habitat	Many areas where there is enough food, water and shade
Food	Long grass, and leaves during dry weather
Predators	Lions and humans
Is it one of the Big Five?	Yes!

Words that appear in the text in bold, **like this**, are explained in the Glossary at the end of this book. Some key words are in colour.

Buffalo come from the same family as cows.

Meet the buffalo

The African buffalo is also called the Cape buffalo. The buffalo comes from the same family as the **domesticated** or **tame** cow. But buffalo are much larger, and they have bigger horns. Both the male and the female buffalo have horns. They also have big, hairy ears that hang down.

Buffalo are known for having a bad temper. They often **charge** at people and other animals, running straight at anyone or anything that gets in their way.

Buffalo are large and dangerous animals, which makes them part of the Big Five group.

Buffalo are large and extremely dangerous animals. For this reason, buffalo are included in the group of animals called the Big Five. The other animals that make up the Big Five are lion, leopard, rhino and elephant. Long ago, people from Europe used to come to Africa to hunt the Big Five. They did this to prove and show how brave they were. Buffalo were often considered the most dangerous of the Big Five to hunt. Nowadays, many people go on holiday to a game reserve to see the Big Five.

All buffalo have horns and a boss, but a female, on the left, has smaller horns and boss than a male, on the right.

Males and females

It is difficult to tell the difference between the male and female buffalo, because they look so much alike. But there are a few ways to tell which is the male buffalo and which is the female.

The older males, called bulls, are black. They often have dried mud on their bodies. This comes from lying in the mud. Bulls have two huge horns that curve up at the ends. Their horns are joined in the middle, sitting on their heads like a helmet. The middle part is the broadest or widest part. We call this broad part of the horns the boss. When buffalo bulls fight, they use their bosses to bash their heads together.

Female buffalo, called cows, are reddish-brown in colour. Their horns and bosses are narrower than the horns and bosses of the bulls.

Young buffalo are brown, and they look similar to the females. But young buffalo have more hair on their bodies than females have. Young bulls even have hair on their bosses. Buffalo lose their hair as they grow older.

Buffalo bulls have huge horns, and often have dried mud on their bodies.

A young buffalo bull, with thinner horns, and hair on his boss.

Buffaloes eat massive amounts of grass.

Food

Animals that eat grass are called grazers. Because buffalo are large animals and eat huge amounts of grass, we call them bulk grazers.

Buffaloes use their large front teeth to cut the grass they eat.

Buffalo eat while they are on the move. They tear off chunks of long grass as they walk through a grassy area. They have a row of large teeth in the front of their mouths and they use them to cut the grass. An antelope, or buck, can tear off a single blade of grass with its lips. Buffalo cannot do this. Their lips are quite stiff and do not move as easily as the lips of antelope move.

Buffalo chew their food loudly. While they are grazing they shuffle through the grass, dragging their hooves along the ground without lifting them very high. Many buffalo together make up what we call a herd. When a herd of buffalo is grazing, the noise of the chewing, together with the noise of the hooves, sounds like a bushfire crackling through dry grass.

Buffalo also **trample** the grass with their hooves. All the grazing and trampling makes the long grass much shorter. In this way, the buffalo prepare the area for animals such as zebra and wildebeest, making it ready for these animals that like to eat shorter grass.

Big herds of buffalo are often very thirsty by the time they reach water, and they go into the water up to their bellies.

Drinking water

Buffalo need to drink a lot of water, which helps them to **digest** the huge amount of long grass that they eat. Special chemicals or juices in their stomachs break the food down so that it can be used by the body. Buffalo usually drink once a day, but in winter, when the weather is dry, they drink at least twice a day.

Buffalo usually move to a waterhole during the late afternoon. They kick up big clouds of dust with their hooves as they rush to the water. People and other animals can see from far away the cloud of dust that the herd makes. A large herd of thirsty buffalo is also noisy.

When buffalo reach the waterhole, they make loud mooing sounds and begin to drink. Some of them walk into the water until they are belly-deep. Buffalo may drink up to 35 litres of water at one time. It takes a buffalo only a few minutes to drink this large amount of water.

Buffalo live in big herds and travel long distances together to find food.

Family life – herds

Buffalo live in big herds. There are between 40 and 100 buffalo in a herd, depending on the season. Males, females, young buffalo and babies all live together in the herd.

In summer, when there is lots of green grass and fresh water, the big herds divide into smaller herds. Sometimes, there are only males in a herd.

It is difficult for buffalo to find food in winter. Often, the best grass is in one place. During the winter months, the smaller herds join up to form one big herd again, to share the grazing. Buffalo are also safer from **predators** when they are in a big group.

Because these buffalo are in a big group, they are safer from predators such as these three lions.

Clans often lie down and sleep together.

Family life – clans

Each large herd of buffalo is made up of smaller groups called clans. The buffalo in a clan all walk together, sleep together and feed together. Every clan has a big bull, which is in charge of the clan. The clan includes mothers, aunts, babies and young bulls. These young bulls stay with the clan for a few years.

When the young bulls become **bachelors**, they are old enough to start mating with female buffalo. The bigger, older bulls then chase the bachelors out of the clan.

Young bulls can only be in charge of a clan once they are seven or eight years old. Before this, they stay together in a group called a **bachelor herd**.

Buffalo bulls dominate the herd.

Who is the boss?

Every clan has a bull that is in charge. There are many clans in a herd of buffalo. This means that there are many bulls in the herd. Bulls are not all equal to one another. Some bulls are more important than others. We call this **rank**. A bull that is older is also bigger, and is usually a strong fighter. Such a bull is a more important bull in the clan, and so he takes charge and **dominates** the other bulls.

Cows also have an order, or rank, in their groups. An older cow dominates over a younger cow. If two cows are the same age but one has a baby, or calf, then she becomes **dominant** over the cow without a calf. But all bulls are senior to cows, which means that they have higher rank than cows.

A dominant buffalo feeds in the front and in the middle of the herd. In front, there is fresh grass, because the grass has not yet been trampled by the other buffaloes' feet. In the middle of the herd, the dominant buffalo is safe from predators such as lions. The animals at the back or at the sides of the group are more likely to be attacked.

Two male buffalo fighting in the Kruger National Park.

Fighting

Buffalo bulls hit their heads together to find out which of them is bigger and stronger. The huge boss in the middle of their horns helps to protect their heads. Their heads crash together with great force, almost like that of a car driving into another car.

Buffalo bulls do not fight each other every time that they meet. They do not forget each other's strength, so the weaker bull will move out of the way of the stronger bull the next time they meet. Sometimes, the bigger bull makes certain signs to remind the weaker buffalo that he is bigger and stronger. This helps to keep the peace in the herd.

When two large males want to mate with the same female, they fight each other until one of them is badly injured or gives up.

A herd being led by path-finder buffaloes.

Finding the way

Buffalo move around all the time, looking for fresh grass and water. A few buffalo in the herd lead the rest of the herd. These buffalo are called path-finders, and they are usually not the dominant buffalo. They just act as leaders of the herd, taking it to places where there is fresh grazing and water.

Some animals, such as lions, have a particular area where they live, called a territory. They protect this territory and do not allow other lions to enter it. Buffalo do not have territories, because they move around all the time. Sometimes they share an area with other herds.

The area where the buffalo herd lives and grazes is called a **home range**. The size of the home range depends on how much food there is. If there is plenty of grass for the buffalo to graze, the home range is smaller. If there is not much grazing, the home range is bigger because the buffalo have to travel further to find it.

A buffalo bull that is old and has left the herd lives near water, where he can wallow in the mud and eat soft grass.

Old buffalo bulls

Old buffalo bulls live alone or in small groups. The small groups usually have two or three buffaloes in them. The buffalo stay close to water at all times, as the grass is softer there. The old buffalo need soft grass to eat because their teeth have become worn down.

The old buffalo spend a lot of time lying in water or rolling in mud. We call this **wallowing**. This helps them to keep cool in hot weather. Wallowing also helps to **soothe** the aches and pains in their old bodies.

The Zulu word for mud is *udaka* (oo-DUH-guh). Because old bulls like wallowing in mud and water, they are sometimes called *dagga*-boys.

Old buffalo bulls are extremely dangerous. They often have skin diseases or old battle wounds. These diseases and injuries are painful and make the bulls bad-tempered. The old bulls do not have the rest of the herd to protect them from lions and so they are aggressive and likely to attack.

Buffalo sniff things that they do not recognise, to find out more about them.

Senses

People, and animals, have five senses: sight, smell, touch, taste and hearing. All five of a buffalo's senses are good, but the sense of smell is best. Buffalo have large noses. They use their sense of smell to find food, and also to find out if predators are nearby.

Buffalo use their sense of smell to stay together in groups. The buffalo in a clan know each other's smell, and this helps them to keep together when they are on the move.

Buffalo have good senses, especially smell and hearing.

Buffalo are **curious** – they are interested in what is going on around them. When they come across something that they do not recognise or know, they move closer to learn more about it. They also stretch out their necks, bringing their noses closer to pick up the smell.

Buffalo also use their sense of hearing to keep in contact with one another while they are on the move. They are noisy animals that bellow, making a louder, deeper sound than the moo of a cow. These noises help the buffalo to stay close together.

On hot days, buffalo like to wallow in a mud bath.

Beating the heat

Buffalo become hot easily. For this reason, they graze early in the morning or late in the afternoon, when the temperature is cooler. In summer the days are extremely hot, so buffalo feed at night when it is much cooler.

During the hottest times of the day, buffalo move into the shade to rest. They also rest at night. When they sleep, they lie with their bodies touching one another for comfort. Resting helps to save their energy. Buffalo need energy to run away from predators such as lions.

Sometimes, buffalo wallow in mud to keep themselves cool. Bulls wallow more than cows. The male buffalo roll in the mud or throw mud around with their horns. They do this to show off and to show how important they are. Mud-wallows are difficult to find and are often small. Only the most important and dominant bulls have a chance to wallow in the mud. And because bulls dominate the cows, cows do not usually have the chance to wallow.

Buffalo chase off two lions by charging at them as a group.

Protecting the herd

When buffalo are scared, they **bellow**. This warns the others in the herd that there is danger. Members of the herd protect and look after one another. The calves and younger animals stay with their mothers. They cluster, staying together in the middle of the herd. The bulls move to the sides and back, to protect the rest of the herd.

Most animals run away quickly from their predators. Buffalo cannot run as fast as many other animals. They run more slowly because they are so big and heavy. Instead, they work as a team. Staying close together, they charge at predators to chase them away. The herd may also **stampede**. The buffalo suddenly start running, and they trample and crush anything that is in their path. Buffalo are usually able to protect the herd. Sometimes they even chase away a pride of lions.

If buffalo flee, or run away, they run at a slow speed so that they can all stay together. But when a single buffalo is charging, it can reach a speed of almost 60 kilometres an hour.

A male buffalo does flehmen, to test if a nearby female is in heat and ready to mate.

Flehmen

When a cow is ready to mate, we say that she is in heat, or in **oestrus** (EE-striss). Buffalo bulls find out if a cow is ready to mate by doing a test called flehmen (FLE-men). Flehmen is a way by which some animals use the top of their mouth to detect and discover smells left by other animals. The word comes from the German word *flehmen*, which means "curling up the upper lip". The bull does flehmen by smelling the urine, or liquid waste matter, that the cow urinates. Then he pulls up his lip and makes a funny face, like a frown. When he lifts his lip, a small hole or gland on the roof of his mouth opens. The gland picks up chemicals in the cow's urine. These chemicals tell the bull if the cow is ready to mate or not.

When a cow is in heat, a bull protects her from other bulls who want to mate with her. The cow does not always want to mate, and she may run away from the protective bull. The noise that she makes when running away attracts and calls other bulls. More dominant bulls will then arrive, and they will chase away the less dominant bulls, until only the strongest and most dominant bull is left. The cow therefore usually mates with the most dominant bull in the group. The bigger and stronger the father is, the bigger and stronger the cow's calf will be.

A young buffalo calf with its mother.

Baby buffalo

Buffalo usually have their calves during summer, when it rains. At this time, there is lots of healthy, green grass for the mothers to eat. Cows need good grazing to make milk for their babies.

Cows give birth in the middle of the herd. This helps to keep the mother and baby safe from predators. But sometimes the cow and her calf are left behind when the herd moves on. This is because the calf is not strong enough to keep up with the bigger buffalo. A calf may stand up ten minutes after it is born, but it cannot run properly until it is a few weeks old.

A newborn buffalo calf.

A red-billed oxpecker looks for parasites on a buffalo's head.

Three yellow-billed oxpeckers on a buffalo's back.

Buffalo and birds

If you see buffalo in the bush, you may notice the birds that usually sit on their backs. These birds are called oxpeckers, and there are two types. Red-billed oxpeckers have completely red beaks. Yellow-billed oxpeckers have some yellow on their beaks.

Oxpeckers peck the ticks from a buffalo's skin. Ticks are parasites. These small creatures bite through the buffalo's skin and suck its blood. By dealing with the ticks, oxpeckers and buffalo help each other: the buffalo are clean and are free of ticks, and the oxpeckers have a meal.

Oxpeckers also help to warn buffalo of danger. When the birds are disturbed by a predator, they fly away, making a lot of noise. The noise tells buffalo that a predator is nearby. The noise also tells humans that there are buffalo close by.

A buffalo cow. She has reddish-brown fur, and her horns are smaller and narrower than a bull's horns.

Glossary

bachelors – males that do not yet have a mate, especially those prevented from breeding by a dominant male

bellow – to make a loud, deep sound

charge – to attack by running straight towards a person or other animal

curious – wanting to know

digest – to break food down in the stomach, so it can be used by the body

domesticated – an animal that is kept by people

dominant – bigger, stronger and more important, and takes charge

dominates – when a bigger, stronger and more important person or animal takes charge of others

home range – the area where buffalo live

oestrus – the times when a female is ready to mate

A buffalo watches a terrapin walk out of a mud-wallow.

Glossary continued

predators – animals that hunt and kill other animals for food

rank – the order of a group and the place that each animal has in that order

soothe – to comfort, and to ease pain

stampede – to suddenly start running as a group

tame – an animal that is not dangerous to people, and is not afraid of people

trample – to walk heavily and squash what the animal walks on

wallowing – lying and rolling around in water and mud

www.ingramcontent.com/pod-product-compliance
Lightning Source LLC
Chambersburg PA
CBHW041323290426

44108CB00004B/113